AMISH

Pies

AMISH
Pies

Traditional Fruit, Nut, Cream, Chocolate, and Custard Pies

Laura Anne Lapp

Photographs by Bonnie Matthews

Good Books

New York, New York

Good Books books may be purchased in bulk at special discounts for sales promotion, corporate gifts, fund-raising, or educational purposes. Special editions can also be created to specifications. For details, contact the Special Sales Department, Good Books, 307 West 36th Street, 11th Floor, New York, NY 10018 or info@skyhorsepublishing.com.

Good Books is an imprint of Skyhorse Publishing, Inc.®, a Delaware corporation.

Visit our website at www.goodbooks.com.

Please follow our publisher Tony Lyons on Instagram @tonylyonsisuncertain.

10 9 8 7 6 5 4 3 2 1

Library of Congress Cataloging-in-Publication Data

Names: Lapp, Laura Anne, author. | Matthews, Bonnie, photographer.
Title: Amish pies : traditional fruit, nut, cream, chocolate, and custard
   pies / Laura Anne Lapp ; photographs by Bonnie Matthews.
Description: New York, NY : Good Books, [2024] | Includes index. | Summary:
   "Sixty sweet and savory authentic Amish pies"-- Provided by publisher.
Identifiers: LCCN 2024013388 (print) | LCCN 2024013389 (ebook) | ISBN
   9781680999273 (paperback) | ISBN 9781680999426 (epub)
Subjects: LCSH: Pies. | Amish cooking. | BISAC: COOKING / Courses & Dishes
   / Pies | COOKING / Comfort Food | LCGFT: Cookbooks.
Classification: LCC TX773 .L298 2024 (print) | LCC TX773 (ebook) | DDC
   641.86/52--dc23/eng/20240327
LC record available at https://lccn.loc.gov/2024013388
LC ebook record available at https://lccn.loc.gov/2024013389

Cover design by Kai Texel
Cover photo by Bonnie Matthews

Print ISBN: 978-1-68099-927-3
Ebook ISBN: 978-1-68099-942-6

Printed in China

CONTENTS

Introduction   vii

Pie Crusts   1

Fruit Pies   15

Nut Pies   61

Cream and Ice Cream Pies   75

Chocolate, Vanilla, Shoofly, and More Pies   97

Savory Pies   125

Index   133

Metric Conversions   137

INTRODUCTION

Pie is a big part of Amish culture. A special dinner or a holiday meal almost always includes pie in the dessert lineup. Pie is also served at church as part of lunch. A typical church lunch is likely to have at least fifteen pies served—sometimes more, if it's a larger community. And no wedding is complete without some kind of pie—often a fancy pie, like coconut cream or peanut butter pie. There are always a few ladies in each community who are known for their pies, and often they bake pies to sell at the market.

In these pages you'll find recipes for pies you're familiar with, such as pumpkin and apple, as well as uniquely Amish pies, such as Snitz, Shoofly, and Vanilla Crumb pies. There are even a few savory pies at the end!

Some Notes on Pie Crust

I've included various recipes for pie dough or crust, but most have many of the same ingredients. There are variations in kinds of shortening, how much water, and whether or not there's sugar or leavening added. Try out the various options until you find the one that works best for you. I've found it takes lots of patience, and then confidence, to perfect pie. I used to always be afraid my pie dough would turn out poorly, but actually, most recipes are forgiving, and if your dough tears while rolling it or placing it in the pan, you can always patch it. Dough that's too dry or has too much flour is very difficult to work with; too wet is easier to remedy than too dry. If you add too much flour, you may have to toss the first batch and start again. Lots of recipes call for pastry flour for pie dough. Sometimes I use that, but if I don't have any, I use all-purpose flour and it works just fine.

It's better to wind up with too much pie dough than too little! You can always trim off the excess from around the rim of your pie plate, sprinkle some cinnamon and sugar on the bits of dough, and bake them in a separate pan for a yummy treat. Let the kids enjoy the baked scraps and maybe they won't dig into the actual pies before they're served! Or if you have way too much dough for the pies you're making, you can roll the extra dough into a ball, wrap it tightly in plastic wrap, and freeze it for later use. You can also roll out additional pie crusts, place them in the pie plates, wrap them entirely in plastic wrap, and freeze them like that.

Transferring Rolled Out Crust to a Pie Plate

Getting your rolled out pie crust into the pie plate without it tearing can be tricky. I always try to roll the bottom crust a bit thicker than the top crust so it's less likely to fall apart as you press it into the pie plate. Try folding the bottom crust in half and then in half again, forming a triangle with one rounded edge. (Be sure your fingers are lightly dusted with flour so they don't stick to the dough.) Then pick up the folded crust, transfer it to the pie plate, and unfold it (see photo on next page). Another option is to roll your crust out between two sheets of parchment paper, then remove the top sheet. You can then invert your pie plate onto the crust, flip the plate and crust over together, and remove the remaining parchment sheet. Or you can try rolling the pie crust up on your rolling pin and then unrolling it into the pie plate.

Speaking of pie plates, you'll want an 8-inch and a 9-inch pie plate—maybe several of each if you'll be baking for a crowd! Glass, Pyrex, or tin all work well.

Blind Baked Pie Crusts

Some recipes call for a pie crust that has already been baked. Pre-baking a pie crust is called blind baking. To do this, place your pie crust in the pie plate and then cover with a large square of parchment paper. Completely cover the bottom surface with a single layer of pie weights, being sure to cover right up to the edges. If you don't have actual pie weights, you can use uncooked rice, dried beans, popcorn kernels, or another pie plate. Bake for 10–15 minutes at 425°F, then remove the weights and parchment paper and bake another 5–7 minutes. Remove from oven and cool on a wire rack.

Pie Crusts

Pie Dough (Variation #1)   **3**

Pie Dough (Variation #2)   **4**

Pie Dough (Variation #3)   **7**

Oatmeal Crust   **8**

Graham Cracker Crust   **10**

Cookie Crust   **13**

PIE DOUGH (VARIATION #1)

Yield: 4 (9-inch) pie crusts (enough for 2 double-crust pies)

Ingredients:

5 cups pastry flour, plus more for dusting
 your work surface
1 tablespoon baking powder
¼ teaspoon salt
2 cups vegetable shortening (I like Crisco)
1 egg
1 tablespoon white vinegar
Water
Egg white or heavy cream
Coarse sanding sugar (optional)

Instructions:

1. Mix dry ingredients in a medium bowl.

2. Add shortening and blend with pastry cutter or a fork until the shortening and flour are combined into coarse crumbs.

3. Whisk the egg and vinegar together in a 1 cup measuring cup and add cold water to equal 1 cup.

4. Carefully pour water over flour mixture, a bit at a time, combining well after each addition.

5. Mix with fork or mixing spoon until you have a uniform ball of dough. Dough should be a little sticky at this point and will not appear perfectly smooth.

6. Sprinkle flour generously on your counter and prepare to roll out the dough. Divide the dough into 4 pieces.

7. Carefully roll one piece of dough into a circular shape, allowing extra dough to drape over the edges of the pan. If the dough is sticky at this point, add flour, lightly dusting the counter and/or the top of the dough.

8. Place dough carefully into the pan, gently pressing on the bottom of the pan and up the sides.

9. If baking a single crust pie, crimp the edges using the tines of a fork, or pinch a V-shape using your thumb and forefinger. Repeat with other crusts, or wrap remaining dough pieces tightly in plastic wrap and freeze for up to six months.

10. After the pie is filled, be sure to moisten the edges of the bottom crust before adding the top layer.

11. Press both layers of pie crust together, again by crimping (see step 9).

12. Brush top crust with beaten egg white or heavy cream to create a nice golden color. Sometimes I sprinkle mine with coarse sanding sugar.

Recipe Note: This is my favorite pie crust recipe. It's super easy to make and very forgiving.

PIE DOUGH (VARIATION #2)

Yield: 1 (10-inch) pie crust, top and bottom

Ingredients:

4 cups all-purpose flour
1 tablespoon sugar
1 teaspoon salt
1 teaspoon baking powder
1¾ cups vegetable shortening
1 tablespoon vinegar
1 egg
½ cup ice water
Egg white or heavy cream
Coarse sanding sugar (optional)

Instructions:

1. Mix dry ingredients in a medium bowl.

2. Add vegetable shortening and blend with pastry cutter or a fork until the vegetable shortening and flour are combined into coarse crumbs.

3. Mix vinegar, egg, and ice water in a small bowl.

4. Carefully pour wet mixture over flour mixture, a bit at a time, combining well after each addition.

5. Mix with fork or mixing spoon until you have a uniform ball of dough. Dough should be a little sticky at this point and will not appear perfectly smooth.

6. Sprinkle flour generously on your counter and prepare to roll out the dough. Divide the dough into 2 pieces.

7. Carefully roll one piece of dough into a circular shape, allowing extra dough to drape over the edges of the pan. If the dough is sticky at this point, add flour, lightly dusting the counter and/or the top of the dough.

8. Place dough carefully into the pan, gently pressing on the bottom of the pan and up the sides.

9. If baking a single crust pie, crimp the edges using the tines of a fork, or pinch a V-shape using your thumb and forefinger. Repeat with other crusts, or wrap remaining dough pieces tightly in plastic wrap and freeze for up to six months.

10. After the pie is filled, be sure to moisten the edges of the bottom crust before adding the top layer.

11. Press both layers of pie crust together, again by crimping (see step 9).

12. Brush top crust with beaten egg white or heavy cream to create a nice golden color. Sometimes I sprinkle mine with coarse sanding sugar.

> *Recipe Note:* This recipe makes a slightly larger crust than what is called for in many recipes. See page vii for an idea for using up excess dough.

PIE DOUGH (VARIATION #3)

Yield: Makes 15 (9-inch) pie crusts, top and bottom

Ingredients:

4 pounds pastry flour
2 pounds bread flour
3 pounds lard or vegetable shortening
1 teaspoon baking soda or
  2 teaspoons baking powder
1 tablespoon salt

Instructions:

1. Blend all ingredients together with pastry cutter or a fork until the vegetable shortening and flour are combined into coarse crumbs. Store in an airtight container for up to a month.

2. When you're ready to bake a pie, follow the directions for Pie Dough Variation 1 (page 3), starting at Step 4 and using approximately 2 cups of crumbs with 1 cup cold water for a bottom crust. Double that to make a top and bottom crust.

Recipe Note: You will need a food scale for this recipe as these measurements are by the pound. This is my Aunt Ruthie's recipe for pie "crumbs." You mix a large quantity of flour, shortening, and leavening and store it in an airtight container for up to several weeks. When you're ready to make a pie, a lot of the work for the crust is already done!

OATMEAL CRUST

Yield: 1 (9-inch) pie crust

Ingredients:

½ cup butter, melted
1 cup oats (quick oats or rolled oats)
½ cup all-purpose flour
2 tablespoons sugar

Instructions:

1. Mix all ingredients together.

2. Pat mixture into bottom and sides of a 9-inch pie plate.

3. Bake at 400°F for 8 to 12 minutes or until golden brown.

Recipe Note: This crust is delicious with fresh strawberry or peach filling topped with whipped cream. When we hosted church services in August one year, I served Fresh Peach Pie (page 25) with this crust. I got tons of compliments.

GRAHAM CRACKER CRUST

Yield: 1 (8-inch) pie crust

Ingredients:

1 sleeve honey graham crackers, crushed
¼–½ cup melted butter
2 teaspoons sugar or
   1 teaspoon cinnamon (optional)

Instructions:

1. In a medium-sized bowl, pour melted butter over crushed graham crackers.

2. Add sugar or cinnamon and stir until combined.

3. Press into 8-inch pie pan.

4. Refrigerate for 15 minutes before filling and baking.

COOKIE CRUST

Yield: 1 (9-inch) pie crust

Ingredients:

1¼–1½ cups cookie crumbs (chocolate wafer, vanilla wafer, or any flavor sandwich crème cookies)
¼ cup or less sugar
¼ cup butter, melted

Instructions:

1. Combine cookie crumbs and sugar.

2. Pour melted butter over crumbs and combine.

3. Press into 9-inch pie pan.

4. Refrigerate 15 minutes.

5. Fill with pudding or similar no-bake filling.

Recipe Note: This is a quick and easy way to make a pie crust for pudding or custard pie, just like the graham cracker crust (page 10), except a slightly different flavor and texture.

Fruit Pies

Apple Pie   **17**

Apple Crumb Pie   **18**

Fresh Fruit Pie   **21**

Fresh Strawberry Pie   **22**

Fresh Peach Pie   **25**

Fresh Blueberry Pie   **26**

French Rhubarb Pie   **29**

Rhubarb Custard Pie   **30**

Lemon Meringue Pie   **33**

Lemon Sponge Pie   **34**

Sour Cream Lemon Pie   **37**

Grandma's Pumpkin Pie   **38**

Pumpkin Pie (Variation #1)   **41**

Pumpkin Pie (Variation #2)   **42**

Pumpkin Pie (Variation #3)   **45**

Layered Pumpkin Pie   **46**

Snitz Pies   **49**

Strawberry Rhubarb Crumb Pie   **50**

Frozen Strawberry Pie (Variation #1)   **53**

Frozen Strawberry Pie (Variation #2)   **54**

Plum Pie   **57**

Pear Pie   **58**

APPLE PIE

Yield: 1 (9-inch) pie

Ingredients:

1 (9-inch) pie crust, top and bottom
3 cups peeled and diced apples
⅔ cup sugar
1 tablespoon all-purpose flour
½ teaspoon cinnamon
2 tablespoons heavy cream

Instructions:

1. Roll out pie crusts and place bottom crust in pie plate.

2. Preheat oven to 400°F.

3. Mix apples, sugar, flour, and cinnamon.

4. Pour mixture into unbaked pie crust.

5. Pour cream over apple mixture.

6. Top with second pie crust or cut strips of dough and make a lattice top.

7. Bake at 400°F for 15 minutes, then reduce heat to 350°F and continue baking for 30 minutes.

Recipe Note: Some Amish women are known in their community for making pies. When church is held in one of their homes, they'll sometimes serve apple pies along with the traditional snitz pies. That's a real treat for everyone!

APPLE CRUMB PIE

Yield: 1 (9-inch) pie

Ingredients:

1 (9-inch) bottom pie crust

Filling:

6 medium apples, diced
1 cup sugar
1 egg, beaten
¼ teaspoon salt
1⅓ cups sour cream
¼ cup all-purpose flour
1 teaspoon vanilla extract
½ teaspoon cinnamon (optional)

Crumbs:

½ cup walnuts or chopped pecans
⅔ cup brown sugar
1 teaspoon cinnamon
½ cup all-purpose flour
½ cup butter, melted

Instructions:

1. Roll out bottom pie crust and place in pie plate.

For the Filling:

1. Preheat oven to 400°F.

2. Mix all Filling ingredients.

3. Pour into unbaked pie crust.

4. Bake at 400°F for 10 minutes. Reduce heat to 350°F and continue baking for 30 minutes.

5. Remove from oven and sprinkle with prepared crumbs.

6. Return to oven and continue baking for 15 minutes.

For the Crumbs:

1. Combine nuts, brown sugar, cinnamon, and flour.

2. Pour melted butter over dry ingredients and combine.

3. Sprinkle over filling.

FRESH FRUIT PIE

Yield: 1 (9-inch) pie

Ingredients:

1 (9-inch) bottom pie crust plus top pie crust or crumb topping of choice
1 cup water
¾ cup sugar
¼ cup Clear-Jel
¼ teaspoon salt
2 teaspoons lemon juice
4 cups fresh fruit (pitted cherries, berries, peaches, pears, etc.)

Instructions:

1. Roll out the bottom pie crust and place in pie plate.

2. In a medium saucepan, combine water, sugar, Clear-Jel, and salt. Heat until thickened.

3. Remove from heat and add lemon juice.

4. Pour fresh fruit into unbaked pie shell. Pour the sugar mixture over the fruit.

5. Top with a second crust, a lattice top, or a crumb topping (page 50).

6. Bake at 350°F for 45 to 60 minutes or until crust is golden brown and filling is bubbling.

7. Cool completely before serving.

FRESH STRAWBERRY PIE

Yield: 1 (8-inch) pie

Ingredients:

1 cup water
1 cup sugar
2 tablespoons cornstarch
1 (3-ounce) box strawberry or raspberry Jell-O
1–1½ quarts fresh strawberries, sliced
1 (8-inch) bottom pie crust or Graham Cracker
    Crust (page 10), baked
Whipped topping (optional)

Instructions:

1. Combine water, sugar, and cornstarch.

2. Bring to a boil over medium heat, stirring until thickened.

3. Remove from heat and add Jell-O.

4. Cool completely and pour over sliced berries.

5. Pour into baked pie crust or graham cracker crust.

6. Top with your choice of whipped topping.

7. Refrigerate until ready to serve.

Recipe Note: Many Amish gardens have a strawberry patch. Mostly we grow strawberry plants so we can make jelly or jam, but fresh strawberry pies are always on the menu in the spring. As long as the berries produce, we'll be serving pie.

FRESH PEACH PIE

Yield: 1 (8-inch) pie

Ingredients:

1 cup water
1 cup sugar
2 tablespoons cornstarch
1 (3-ounce) box peach or apricot Jell-O
1–1½ quarts fresh peaches, sliced
1 (8-inch) bottom pie crust or Graham Cracker
   Crust (page 10), baked
Whipped topping (optional)

Instructions:

1. Combine water, sugar, and cornstarch.

2. Bring to a boil over medium heat, stirring until thickened.

3. Remove from heat and add Jell-O.

4. Cool completely and pour over sliced peaches.

5. Pour into baked pie crust or graham cracker crust.

6. Top with your choice of whipped topping.

7. Refrigerate until ready to serve.

Recipe Note: This pie is simple and delicious, especially on warm days. The glaze can be made up to 1 week in advance and stored in the refrigerator.

FRESH BLUEBERRY PIE

Yield: 1 (8-inch) pie

Ingredients:

3 tablespoons sugar
2 tablespoons all-purpose flour
2 cups sour cream
1 egg, beaten
½ cup sugar
2 cups blueberries, fresh
1 graham cracker crust, unbaked (page 10)

Instructions:

1. Preheat oven to 400°F.

2. Mix 3 tablespoons sugar with the flour.

3. Stir in sour cream and egg.

4. In a separate bowl, combine sugar and blueberries.

5. Spoon half of sour cream mixture into the pie crust.

6. Pour blueberries on top of sour cream mixture.

7. Top with remaining sour cream mixture.

8. Bake at 400°F for 10 to 15 minutes or until filling is set.

9. Chill until ready to serve.

FRENCH RHUBARB PIE

Yield: 1 (9-inch) pie

Ingredients:

1 (9-inch) bottom pie crust

Filling:

1 egg
1 cup sugar
1 teaspoon vanilla extract
2 cups diced rhubarb
2 tablespoons all-purpose flour

Crumb Topping:

½ cup brown sugar
¾ cup all-purpose flour
⅓ cup butter

Instructions:

1. Roll out pie crust and place in pie plate.

2. Mix all Filling ingredients together and pour into prepared pie crust.

3. Combine Crumb Topping ingredients.

4. Sprinkle Crumb Topping over fruit filling.

5. Bake at 400°F for 10 minutes. Reduce heat to 350°F and continue baking for 30 minutes.

RHUBARB CUSTARD PIE

Yield: 1 (9-inch) pie

Ingredients:

1 (9-inch) bottom pie crust
2 cups diced rhubarb
¾ cup sugar
2 tablespoons all-purpose flour
2 eggs, separated
2 tablespoons butter, melted
1 teaspoon vanilla extract
1 cup half-and-half
¼ cup sugar (for meringue topping)

Instructions:

1. Roll out pie crust and place in pie plate.

2. Preheat oven to 350°F.

3. Place diced rhubarb in pie crust.

4. Combine sugar, flour, egg yolks, melted butter, and vanilla extract. Mix well.

5. Heat half-and-half until warm and add to sugar mixture.

6. Pour mixture over rhubarb.

7. Bake for 45 minutes at 350°F. Remove from oven, but leave oven on.

8. To make the meringue, whip two reserved egg whites with ¼ cup sugar.

9. Spread meringue on top of pie and return to oven until top is golden brown, 10 to 15 minutes.

LEMON MERINGUE PIE

Yield: 1 (9-inch) pie

Ingredients:

1 (9-inch) pie crust, baked

Filling:
8 large eggs, divided
1 cup sugar
¾ cup lemon juice
2 tablespoons cornstarch
½ cup butter, diced

Meringue:
½ teaspoon cornstarch
¼ teaspoon cream of tartar
½ cup sugar
1 teaspoon vanilla extract

Instructions:

1. Roll out pie crust and place in pie plate.

2. Combine four egg yolks (reserving egg whites for the meringue), four whole eggs, sugar, lemon juice, and cornstarch.

3. Heat on stovetop until thickened, stirring occasionally.

4. Remove from heat and stir in butter.

5. Pour into crust and top with Meringue (directions follow).

6. To make the Meringue, beat the 4 reserved egg whites until foamy.

7. Beat in cornstarch and cream of tartar.

8. Slowly add sugar and vanilla extract (a little at a time), beating continuously until stiff peaks form.

9. Spoon Meringue over pie, making sure Filling is covered.

10. Bake at 350°F 10 to 15 minutes or until Meringue is golden and toasty.

LEMON SPONGE PIE

Yield: 1 (9-inch) pie

Ingredients:

1 (9-inch) bottom piecrust
1 cup sugar
2½ tablespoons all-purpose flour
2 eggs, separated
1 tablespoon lemon juice
1 tablespoon butter, melted
1 cup milk

Instructions:

1. Roll out pie crust and place in pie plate.

2. Combine sugar and flour.

3. In a separate bowl, mix egg yolks (reserving the whites), lemon juice, melted butter, and milk.

4. Stir dry ingredients into egg mixture.

5. Beat egg whites until stiff peaks form and fold into filling.

6. Pour into unbaked pie crust and bake at 375°F for 45 to 55 minutes or until golden brown.

Recipe Note: Grandma was always happy to make this old-fashioned lemon pie for my sister. Sponge or custard pies are popular at Amish weddings as a dessert option, perhaps because they seem a little fancier than regular fruit pies.

SOUR CREAM LEMON PIE

Yield: 1 (9-inch) pie

Ingredients:

1 cup sugar
3 tablespoons cornstarch
1 cup milk
⅓ cup lemon juice
1 tablespoon lemon zest, plus more for garnish
2 tablespoons butter
¾ cup sour cream
1 (9-inch) pie crust, baked
Whipped cream, for serving

Instructions:

1. Combine sugar, cornstarch, milk, lemon juice, and lemon zest. Whisk over medium heat until thickened.

2. Remove from heat and stir in butter.

3. Cool to room temperature and stir in sour cream.

4. Pour into baked pie crust and top with whipped cream.

5. Garnish with lemon zest.

GRANDMA'S PUMPKIN PIE

Yield: 3 (10-inch) pies

Ingredients:

3 (10-inch) bottom pie crusts
2½ cups white sugar
2 tablespoons all-purpose flour
3 teaspoons cinnamon
1 teaspoon salt
2½ cups pumpkin purée
6 eggs, separated
2 cans evaporated milk
3 cups milk, hot (but not boiling)
1 tablespoon vanilla extract

Instructions:

1. Preheat oven to 425°F.

2. Roll out pie crusts and place in pie plates.

3. Mix together sugar, flour, cinnamon, and salt.

4. In a separate bowl, combine pumpkin, egg yolks (reserving egg whites), evaporated milk, and hot milk.

5. Stir wet mixture into dry ingredients.

6. Whip egg whites until soft peaks form.

7. Fold beaten egg whites and vanilla extract into pumpkin mixture.

8. Pour into prepared pie crusts.

9. Bake at 425°F for 10 minutes. Reduce heat to 350°F and continue baking 30 to 35 minutes or until golden brown.

10. Remove from oven before center is completely set. Grandma always said, it should be a bit wobbly!

Recipe Note: These are my favorite pumpkin pies. It's the first pie recipe I ever tried, and Grandma was so proud to share it with me. Grandma was a wonderful cook and I owe my skills to the helpful recipes and tips that she shared with me. I miss asking her questions and hope she knew how much I appreciated her help. I still cherish the hand-written recipes and letters that she mailed to me.

PUMPKIN PIE (VARIATION #1)

Yield: 2 (9-inch) pies

Ingredients:

2 (9-inch) bottom pie crusts
1 cup sugar
1 tablespoon all-purpose flour
1 tablespoon cornstarch
½ teaspoon salt
¼ teaspoon allspice
1 teaspoon cinnamon
2 tablespoons molasses
2 eggs, separated
2 cups milk
1½ cups pumpkin purée

Instructions:

1. Roll out two bottom pie crusts and place in pie plates.

2. Preheat oven to 450°F.

3. Combine all ingredients except egg whites.

4. Whip egg whites until soft peaks form. Fold whipped egg whites into pumpkin mixture.

5. Pour into prepared pie crusts.

6. Bake at 450°F for 10 minutes.

7. Reduce heat to 350°F and continue baking for 30 minutes or until golden brown.

Recipe Note: Most pumpkin pie recipes are similar to each other, but there are little tweaks here and there. Variations in ingredients, mostly, but sometimes in the techniques as well, like adding egg whites last, heating the milk . . . just little things like that. It seems like each baker has their own secret touch. And inevitably each one thinks their recipe is the best!

PUMPKIN PIE (VARIATION #2)

Yield: 2 (9-inch) pies

Ingredients:

2 (9-inch) bottom pie crusts
6 eggs
1½ cups sugar
1½ cups brown sugar
1 teaspoon nutmeg
1 tablespoon all-purpose flour
½ teaspoon salt
1 teaspoon cinnamon
¼ teaspoon ginger
4 cups pumpkin
2 cans evaporated milk

Instructions:

1. Roll out two bottom pie crusts and place in pie plates.

2. Preheat oven to 425°F.

3. Beat eggs, then add remaining ingredients, stirring well.

4. Add evaporated milk.

5. Pour into prepared pie crusts.

6. Bake for 15 minutes. Reduce heat to 350°F and continue baking 30 minutes or until golden brown.

PUMPKIN PIE (VARIATION #3)

Yield: 2 pies

Ingredients:

2 (9-inch) bottom pie crusts
3 eggs, separated
1 cup sugar
1 cup brown sugar
1 cup pumpkin
3 tablespoons all-purpose flour
1 teaspoon salt
1½ teaspoons nutmeg (optional)
1 teaspoon cinnamon
3 cups milk, heated (hot, but not boiling)

Instructions:

1. Roll out two bottom pie crusts and place in pie plates.

2. Preheat oven to 425°F.

3. Beat egg yolks (reserving the whites) and sugar until light and fluffy.

4. Add remaining ingredients, except egg whites.

5. Beat egg whites until fluffy and fold into mixture.

6. Pour into prepared pie crusts.

7. Bake at 425°F for 10 minutes.

8. Reduce heat to 350°F and continue baking for 30 minutes or until golden brown.

Recipe Note: Often in the fall we'll serve pumpkin pie as part of our church lunch. This is one of our church lady's favorite recipes. Her pumpkin pies are some of the best.

LAYERED PUMPKIN PIE

———————

Yield: 2 (9-inch) pies

Ingredients:

2 (9-inch) bottom pie crusts

Syrup for Bottom Layer:

1 cup water
½ cup brown sugar
2 tablespoons all-purpose flour
1 cup molasses
1 egg
1 teaspoon baking soda

Topping:

1 cup sugar
2 eggs
2 teaspoons cinnamon
1 teaspoon baking powder
½ teaspoon salt
1 cup all-purpose flour
1 cup pumpkin purée
⅓ cup vegetable oil
1 teaspoon baking soda

Instructions:

1. Preheat oven to 350°F. Roll out two bottom pie crusts and place in pie plates.

2. Mix all ingredients for Syrup and pour into prepared pie crusts.

3. Mix ingredients for Topping, combining well.

4. Spoon Topping over Syrup.

5. Bake at 350°F for 50 minutes or until golden brown.

SNITZ PIES

Yield: 10 pies

Ingredients:

20 pie crusts (10 top and 10 bottom)
1 gallon applesauce (sweetened)
1 pound sugar
1 pound brown sugar
½ cup granulated tapioca
1–2 teaspoons cinnamon
½ teaspoon salt

Instructions:

1. Roll out bottom crusts and place in pie plates.

2. Stir together all remaining ingredients until smooth.

3. Pour filling into prepared bottom pie crusts, cover with top crusts, and bake at 350°F for about 45 minutes.

Recipe Notes: The following recipe is for a bulk batch of snitz pie filling. If you're not planning to make several pies at once, you can can or freeze the filling for later use.

The recipe for snitz pies is a large recipe because, typically, the only time we make snitz pies is for church. Amish families take turns hosting church services in their homes. Services begin at 8:00am and last for 3 hours. After services, there's a light lunch served, which always consists of sliced homemade bread with cheese and peanut butter spread, pickled beets and pickles, and usually sliced bologna or deli ham. And there's always pie. Most times snitz pie, but occasionally pumpkin in the fall, or in the warm summer months we sometimes have fresh peach or strawberry pie.

STRAWBERRY RHUBARB CRUMB PIE

Yield: 1 (9-inch) pie

Ingredients:

1 (9-inch) bottom pie crust
1 egg, beaten
2 tablespoons all-purpose flour
1¼ cups sugar
1 teaspoon vanilla extract
3 cups chopped rhubarb
2 cups diced strawberries

Crumb Topping:

¾ cup all-purpose flour
½ cup oatmeal
½ cup brown sugar
½ cup butter

Instructions:

1. Roll out bottom pie crust and place in pie plate.

2. Preheat oven to 400°F.

3. Combine egg, flour, sugar, and vanilla extract.

4. Gently fold in fresh fruit.

5. Pour into prepared pie crust.

6. Mix all the Crumb Topping ingredients together until crumbly. Sprinkle evenly over top of the pie.

7. Bake at 400°F for 10 minutes.

8. Reduce heat to 350°F and continue baking for 35 minutes or until crumbs are golden brown.

FROZEN STRAWBERRY PIE (VARIATION #1)

Yield: 2 (9-inch) pies

Ingredients:

Crust:
1 cup peanut butter
1 cup corn syrup
2 cups crispy rice cereal

Filling:
1 cup sugar
2 cups crushed strawberries
2 egg whites, beaten
2 cups whipped topping

Instructions:

1. Mix all the Crust ingredients together and press into pie pan.

2. Mix sugar and strawberries.

3. In a separate bowl, whip egg whites.

4. Fold whipped egg whites and whipped topping into the sugared strawberries.

5. Pour mixture into the crust. Cover and freeze for 3 hours.

Recipe Note: This pie is also delicious with a Graham Cracker Crust (page 10).

FROZEN STRAWBERRY PIE (VARIATION #2)

Yield: 2 (8-inch) pies

Ingredients:

2 prepared pie crusts (chocolate cookie, page 13, or graham cracker, page 10)

Filling:

8 ounces softened cream cheese
1 cup sugar
1 teaspoon vanilla extract
4 cups chopped strawberries
2 cups whipped topping

Instructions:

1. Mix cream cheese, sugar, and vanilla extract.

2. Stir in strawberries and whipped topping.

3. Pour into crusts.

4. Freeze for 3 hours before serving.

PLUM PIE

Yield: 1 (9-inch) pie

Ingredients:

Filling:
1 (9-inch) bottom pie crust, unbaked
4 cups sliced, fresh plums
½ cup sugar
¼ cup all-purpose flour
½ teaspoon salt
¼ teaspoon cinnamon
1 tablespoon lemon juice

Topping:
½ cup sugar
½ cup all-purpose flour
¼ teaspoon cinnamon
3 tablespoons butter

Instructions:

1. Roll out pie crust and place in pie plate.

2. Preheat oven to 375°F.

3. Mix all Filling ingredients and pour into pie crust.

4. Mix Topping ingredients until coarse crumbs form.

5. Sprinkle Topping over Filling.

6. Bake at 375°F for 50 minutes or until bubbly and golden brown.

PEAR PIE

Yield: 2 (8-inch) pies

Ingredients:

2 (8-inch) bottom piecrusts, unbaked

Filling:
¾ cup brown sugar
2 tablespoons cornstarch
1 teaspoon cinnamon
½ teaspoon salt
6 cups fresh, peeled and diced pears
1 tablespoon lemon juice

Crumbs:
6 tablespoons softened butter
¾ cup all-purpose flour
½ cup brown sugar

Instructions:

1. Roll out the pie crusts and place them in two pie plates.

2. Preheat oven to 400°F.

3. Mix all ingredients for Filling.

4. Divide Filling evenly between two pie crusts.

5. Mix Crumbs ingredients together and sprinkle them over the Filling.

6. Bake at 400°F for 1 hour or until golden brown.

Nut Pies

Pecan Pie (Variation #1)   **63**

Grandma's Pecan Pie (Variation #2)   **64**

Pecan Pie (Variation #3)   **67**

Easy Peanut Butter Pie   **68**

Peanut Butter Pie with Chocolate Crust   **71**

Peanut Butter Cup Pie   **72**

PECAN PIE (VARIATION #1)

Yield: 1 (9-inch) pie

Ingredients:

1 (9-inch) bottom pie crust, unbaked

Filling:

1 cup corn syrup
½ cup sugar
3 tablespoons butter, melted
¼ teaspoon salt
3 eggs, beaten
1 teaspoon vanilla extract
1 cup pecans

Instructions:

1. Roll out bottom pie crust and place in pie plate.

2. Preheat oven to 350°F.

3. Mix all Filling ingredients.

4. Pour into unbaked pie crust.

5. Bake at 350°F for 45 minutes.

Recipe Note: This pecan pie recipe varies just slightly from the next two on the following pages. Can you taste a difference? It's nice to have various recipes to choose from, even if the differences are very subtle.

GRANDMA'S PECAN PIE (VARIATION #2)

Yield: 1 (9-inch) pie

Ingredients:

1 (9-inch) bottom pie crust, unbaked

Filling:

¼ cup butter, melted
⅔ cup brown sugar
⅔ cup corn syrup
1 tablespoon all-purpose flour
½ cup water
3 eggs, beaten
1 teaspoon vanilla extract
1 cup pecans

Instructions:

1. Roll out pie crust and place in pie plate.

2. Preheat oven to 350°F.

3. In a medium bowl, combine all Filling ingredients except pecans.

4. Sprinkle pecans evenly over bottom of pie crust.

5. Carefully pour Filling on top (pecans will float to the top).

6. Bake at 350°F for 35 minutes.

Recipe Note: This is another recipe from my Grandma. Her pecan pie was wonderful, and she was so proud of it!

PECAN PIE (VARIATION #3)

Yield: 1 (9-inch) pie

Ingredients:

1 (9-inch) pie crust, unbaked
¾ cup sugar
¾ cup corn syrup
2 eggs
2 tablespoons heavy cream
1 tablespoon all-purpose flour
¼ teaspoon salt
¾ cup water
1 cup pecans

Instructions:

1. Roll out pie crust and place in pie plate.

2. Preheat oven to 350°F.

3. Beat together sugar, corn syrup, eggs, cream, flour, and salt.

4. Stir in water and pecans.

5. Pour into unbaked pie crust.

6. Bake at 350°F for 45 minutes.

EASY PEANUT BUTTER PIE

Yield: 1 (8-inch) pie

Ingredients:

1 graham cracker crust, baked (page 10)
8 ounces cream cheese, softened
1 cup powdered sugar
½ cup peanut butter
8 ounces whipped topping, plus more for serving
½ cup milk

Instructions:

1. Mix all ingredients and pour into prepared pie crust.

2. Top with whipped topping.

3. Chill for 2 hours before serving.

Recipe Note: There are many variations of peanut butter pie. Most are a cold, creamy version of peanut butter pudding or custard and all are topped with heavy whipping cream or whipped topping. All of the fillings and crusts can be interchangeable to make your own "best" peanut butter pie. This first variation is one of the easiest and can be topped with whipped topping or whipped cream, or simply peanut butter crumbs made by mixing equal amounts of powdered sugar and peanut butter.

PEANUT BUTTER PIE WITH CHOCOLATE CRUST

Yield: 1 (9-inch) pie

Ingredients:

Crust:
1½ cups chocolate cookie crumbs
¼ cup sugar
½ cup butter, melted

Filling:
8 ounces cream cheese
1 cup peanut butter
1 cup sugar
1 teaspoon vanilla extract
1 tablespoon butter, softened
1 cup whipped cream

Instructions:

1. Mix Crust ingredients and press into pie pan.

2. Chill for 15 minutes.

3. Combine all Filling ingredients.

4. Pour into pie crust.

5. Chill for 2 hours before serving.

PEANUT BUTTER CUP PIE

Yield: 1 (9-inch) pie

Ingredients:

1 (9-inch) bottom pie crust, unbaked

Bottom Layer:
½ cup sugar
1 tablespoon all-purpose flour
2 tablespoons baking cocoa
¼ cup milk
1 egg, beaten
1 teaspoon vanilla extract

Filling:
4 ounces cream cheese
1 cup whipped topping
¼ cup peanut butter
½ cup powdered sugar
½ teaspoon vanilla extract

Garnish:
Chocolate bar, cut into bits, *or*
Peanut butter cups, cut into bits

Instructions:

1. Roll out crust and place in pie plate.
2. Preheat oven to 350°F.
3. Mix all ingredients for Bottom Layer.
4. Pour into pie crust and bake for 20 minutes.
5. Chill.
6. Mix all Filling ingredients.
7. Pour over Bottom Layer.
8. Garnish with chocolate bits or chopped peanut butter cups.
9. Chill for 2 hours before serving.

Cream and Ice Cream Pies

Sour Cream Pear Pie **77**

Pear Custard Pie **78**

Peaches and Cream Pie **81**

Raspberry Swirl Pie **82**

Raisin Crème Pie (Variation #1) **85**

Raisin Crème Pie (Variation #2) **86**

Maple Cream Pie **89**

Cream Cheese Pecan Pie **90**

Ice Cream "Pie" with Peanut Butter Crust **93**

Cappuccino Ice Cream Pie **94**

SOUR CREAM PEAR PIE

Yield: 1 (9-inch) pie

Ingredients:

1 (9-inch) bottom pie crust

Filling:

2 cups peeled, chopped pears
½–¾ cup sugar
1 egg, beaten
1½ tablespoons all-purpose flour
1 cup sour cream
1 teaspoon vanilla extract
¼ teaspoon salt

Crumb Topping:

½ cup sugar
⅓ cup all-purpose flour
¼ cup butter, softened

Instructions:

1. Roll out bottom pie crust and place in a pie plate.

2. Preheat oven to 350°F.

3. Mix all Filling ingredients and pour into pie crust.

4. Bake for 25 minutes at 350°F.

5. Mix together Crumb Topping ingredients.

6. Sprinkle over Filling.

7. Continue baking at 350°F for 30 minutes or until golden brown.

PEAR CUSTARD PIE

Yield: 1 (9-inch) pie

Ingredients:

Crust:
½ cup butter, room temperature
½ cup sugar
¾ cup all-purpose flour
½ teaspoon vanilla extract

Filling:
8 ounces cream cheese, room temperature
½ cup sugar
1 egg
1 teaspoon vanilla extract

2 cups peeled, diced pears

Topping:
1 teaspoon sugar
1 teaspoon cinnamon

Instructions:

1. Preheat oven to 375°F.

2. Mix Crust ingredients and press into a 9-inch pie pan.

3. Bake for 15 minutes or until lightly browned. Cool completely.

4. Mix cream cheese, sugar, egg, and vanilla extract. Pour over Crust.

5. Sprinkle pears over Filling.

6. Mix sugar and cinnamon and sprinkle over pears.

7. Bake at 375°F for 30 minutes.

8. Cool and refrigerate at least 2 hours before serving.

PEACHES AND CREAM PIE

Yield: 1 (9-inch) pie

Ingredients:

¾ cup all-purpose flour
1 teaspoon baking powder
3 tablespoons butter (room temperature)
1 egg
½ cup milk
1 (3.4-ounce) package cook & serve vanilla pudding
1 (15.3-ounce) can sliced peaches

Topping:

8 ounces cream cheese
½ cup sugar
3 tablespoons peach juice

Instructions:

1. Preheat oven to 350°F.

2. Mix flour, baking powder, butter, egg, milk, and pudding mix.

3. Spread into greased 10-inch pie pan.

4. Cover with drained, chopped peaches, reserving the peach juice.

5. Mix Topping ingredients and spread over peaches.

6. Bake at 350°F for 35 minutes.

RASPBERRY SWIRL PIE

Yield: 1 (9-inch) pie

Ingredients:

Filling:
Graham cracker crust (page 10)
8 ounces cream cheese, room temperature
1 (14-ounce) can sweetened condensed milk
1 egg
3 tablespoons lemon juice
¾ cup raspberry or strawberry jam

Instructions:

1. Preheat oven to 300°F.

2. In a large bowl, combine all Filling ingredients except jam.

3. Pour half the Filling into the crust.

4. Pour half the jam over the Filling.

5. Pour remaining Filling over jam.

6. Swirl remaining jam over top layer of Filling.

7. Bake at 300°F for 55 minutes.

8. Cool completely before serving.

RAISIN CRÈME PIE (VARIATION #1)

Yield: 1 (9-inch) pie

Ingredients:

1 (9-inch) bottom pie crust, baked
2 cups milk
1 cup sugar
2 egg yolks
4 tablespoons all-purpose flour
1 tablespoon butter
1 cup raisins, cooked in water for 5 minutes and
  drained
Whipped topping, for serving

Instructions:

1. In medium saucepan, bring milk to a boil.

2. Mix sugar, egg yolks, flour, and butter along with a little of the hot milk.

3. Add to remaining milk and cook until thickened.

4. Add raisins.

5. Pour into pie crust.

6. Cool.

7. Serve with whipped topping.

Recipe Note: This recipe and the next are very similar, but this one uses flour instead of cornstarch, which results in a slightly different texture. Variation #2 also includes nuts, whereas this recipe sticks with just the raisins.

RAISIN CREAM PIE (VARIATION #2)

Yield: 1 (9-inch) pie

Ingredients:

1 (9-inch) pie crust, baked
2 tablespoons cornstarch
1 cup sugar
2 egg yolks
1½ cups milk
1 cup raisins
1 tablespoon butter
1 teaspoon vanilla extract
Crushed pecans or walnuts
Whipped cream, for serving

Instructions:

1. In a small bowl, pour boiling water over raisins and allow to sit.

2. Stir together cornstarch, sugar, egg yolks, and milk.

3. Heat over medium heat, stirring until thickened.

4. Drain raisins and add to filling, along with butter, vanilla extract, and nuts.

5. Pour into pie crust.

6. Cool.

7. Top with whipped cream.

Recipe Note: If you're making your own whipped cream to serve with the pie, try adding a bit of maple syrup to sweeten it.

MAPLE CREAM PIE

Yield: 1 (8-inch) pie

Ingredients:

1 (8-inch) bottom pie crust or graham cracker
  crust, baked

Filling:

1¼ cups milk
¼ cup cornstarch
½ cup maple syrup
2 egg yolks
2 tablespoons melted butter
Crushed pecans or walnuts (optional)
1 cup whipped cream (plus more for topping)

Instructions:

1. Combine all Filling ingredients except whipped cream.

2. Heat over medium heat, until thickened, stirring often.

3. Remove from heat and cool.

4. Fold in whipped cream.

5. Pour into pie crust.

6. Top with whipped cream.

Recipe Note: If you're making your own whipped cream to serve with the pie, try sweetening it with a bit of maple syrup.

CREAM CHEESE PECAN PIE

Yield: 1 (9-inch) pie

Ingredients:

1 (9-inch) bottom pie crust, unbaked
8 ounces cream cheese, room temperature
1 egg, beaten
1 teaspoon vanilla extract
½ cup sugar
¼ teaspoon salt
1 cup pecans

Topping:

3 eggs
1 cup corn syrup
1 teaspoon vanilla extract

Instructions:

1. Roll out pie crust and place in pie plate.

2. Preheat oven to 375°F.

3. Mix cream cheese, egg, vanilla extract, sugar, and salt.

4. Spread in bottom of pie crust.

5. Sprinkle with pecans.

6. Combine Topping ingredients and beat well.

7. Pour over pecans.

8. Bake at 375°F for 45 minutes or until golden brown.

ICE CREAM "PIE" WITH PEANUT BUTTER CRUST

Yield: 1 (9-inch) pie

Ingredients:

¾ cup peanut butter

2 cups crispy rice cereal

Ice cream of your choice

Topping of your choice (fudge or caramel syrup, chopped nuts or candy pieces, sprinkles etc.)

Instructions:

1. Mix peanut butter and crispy rice cereal.

2. Press into 9-inch pie pan.

3. Fill pan with ice cream, slightly softened.

4. Add any toppings.

Recipe Note: Ice cream "pie" is a super quick and easy dessert. It tastes great on a hot afternoon, or makes the best dessert after a dinner of corn-on-the-cob. It's the perfect ending for any summer meal!

CAPPUCCINO ICE CREAM PIE

Yield: 1 (8-inch) pie

Ingredients:

1 graham cracker crust, baked and cooled (page 10)
½ cup fudge topping, warmed slightly
1 quart ice cream, slightly softened
1 tablespoon instant coffee dissolved in
   1 teaspoon hot water
1 teaspoon cinnamon (optional)
Whipped topping, for serving
Chopped nuts, for garnish (optional)

Instructions:

1. Spread fudge over the graham cracker crust.

2. Combine ice cream, coffee, and cinnamon.

3. Pour into pie crust.

4. Freeze for 3 hours.

5. Serve with whipped topping. If desired, garnish with chopped nuts.

Chocolate, Vanilla, Shoofly, and More Pies

Chocolate Pie **99**

Chocolate Chess Pie **100**

Chocolate Chip Cookie Pie **103**

Vanilla Pie **104**

Vanilla Crumb Pie **107**

Shoofly Pie (Variation #1) **108**

Shoofly Pie (Variation #2) **111**

Chocolate Shoofly Pie **112**

Butterscotch Pie **115**

Oatmeal Pie **116**

Coconut Oatmeal Pie **119**

Sweet Potato Pie (Variation #1) **120**

Sweet Potato Pie (Variation #2) **123**

CHOCOLATE PIE

Yield: 1 (8-inch) pie

Ingredients:

1 bottom (8-inch) pie crust or graham cracker crust, baked

Filling:

1 cup sugar
1½ tablespoons cocoa
2 tablespoons cornstarch
¼ teaspoon salt
2 cups milk
1 teaspoon vanilla extract
3 tablespoons butter, melted

Topping:

Whipped topping, for serving

Instructions:

1. Mix all ingredients for Filling.

2. Heat over medium heat, stirring often, until thickened.

3. Pour into pie crust.

4. Chill for at least an hour.

5. Add whipped topping before serving.

CHOCOLATE CHESS PIE

Yield: 1 (9-inch) pie

Ingredients:

Filling:

1 (9-inch) bottom pie crust, unbaked
1¼ cups sugar
3½ tablespoons cocoa
2 eggs, beaten
¼ cup butter, melted
1 (5.33-ounce) can evaporated milk
1 teaspoon vanilla extract
½ cup walnuts or nuts of your choice

Instructions:

1. Roll out pie crust and place in pie plate.

2. Preheat oven to 350°F.

3. Mix all Filling ingredients except nuts.

4. Pour into pie crust.

5. Sprinkle with nuts.

6. Bake at 350°F for 50 minutes.

Recipe Note: Chocolate Chess Pie and Chocolate Chip Cookie Pie (page 103) are basically cookies in a pie crust. They're easy to make and kids love them!

CHOCOLATE CHIP COOKIE PIE

Yield: 1 (9-inch) pie

Ingredients:

1 (9-inch) bottom pie crust, unbaked

Filling:

¾ cup butter, melted
2 eggs, beaten
¾ cup all-purpose flour
½ cup sugar
⅓ cup brown sugar
1 cup chocolate chips
½ cup nuts (optional)

Instructions:

1. Roll out bottom pie crust and place in pie plate.

2. Preheat oven to 325°F.

3. Mix all Filling ingredients.

4. Pour into pie crust.

5. Bake at 325°F for 1 hour.

VANILLA PIE

Yield: 1 (8-inch) pie

Ingredients:

1 (8-inch) bottom pie crust, unbaked

Filling:

½ cup brown sugar
½ cup molasses
1½ tablespoons all-purpose flour
1¼ cups water
1 teaspoon vanilla extract

Crumbs:

½ cup all-purpose flour
¼ cup brown sugar
2 tablespoons shortening or butter
¼ teaspoon baking soda
¼ teaspoon baking powder

Instructions:

1. Roll out pie crust and place in pie plate.

2. Preheat oven to 375°F.

3. Mix all Filling ingredients and heat over medium heat, stirring often until thickened.

4. Cool and pour into pie crust.

5. Mix Crumbs ingredients.

6. Sprinkle over Filling.

7. Bake at 375°F for 40 minutes or until golden brown.

Recipe Note: Vanilla pies are very traditional crumb pies and are often served at weddings.

VANILLA CRUMB PIE

Yield: 1 (9-inch) pie

Ingredients:

1 (9-inch) bottom pie shell, unbaked

Filling:

1 cup brown sugar
2½ tablespoons all-purpose flour
1 cup corn syrup
2 cups hot water
1 teaspoon vanilla extract

Crumbs:

2 cups all-purpose flour
1 teaspoon baking soda
1 teaspoon cream of tartar
1 cup brown sugar
½ cup butter

Instructions:

1. Roll out pie crust and place in pie plate.

2. Preheat oven to 400°F.

3. Combine all Filling ingredients.

4. Pour into pie crust and allow to cool.

5. Mix Crumbs.

6. Sprinkle Crumbs over Filling.

7. Bake at 400°F for 10 minutes, reduce heat to 350°F, and continue baking for 35 minutes or until nicely browned.

SHOOFLY PIE (VARIATION #1)

Yield: 1 (10-inch) pie

Ingredients:

1 (10-inch) bottom pie crust, unbaked

Crumbs:
3 cups all-purpose flour
1 cup brown sugar
½ cup vegetable shortening
½ teaspoon baking soda

Filling:
1½ cups molasses
1½ cups hot water
¾ teaspoon baking soda
½ cup brown sugar
3 eggs, beaten
¼ teaspoon cinnamon

Instructions:

1. Roll out bottom pie crust and place in pie plate.

2. Preheat oven to 350°F.

3. Mix all Crumbs ingredients until coarse crumbs form.

4. In a separate bowl, combine all Filling ingredients and mix well.

5. Add 1½ cups Crumbs to Filling mixture. Reserve remaining crumbs for topping.

6. Pour Filling into unbaked pie crust.

7. Top with remaining Crumbs.

8. Bake at 350°F for 45 minutes.

Recipe Note: This Shoofly Pie variation has a hint of cinnamon in the sweet molasses filling. Note that this recipe makes one pie and the recipe on page 111 makes two pies. Also check out Chocolate Shoofly Pie on page 112.

SHOOFLY PIE (VARIATION #2)

Yield: 2 (9-inch) pies

Ingredients:

2 (9-inch) bottom pie crusts, unbaked

Filling:
1 teaspoon baking soda
2 cups hot water
2 cups molasses
2 eggs, beaten
½ cup brown sugar

Crumbs:
6 cups all-purpose flour
2 cups brown sugar
1 cup vegetable shortening
1 teaspoon baking soda
½ teaspoon salt

Instructions:

1. Preheat oven to 350°F.

2. Dissolve baking soda in hot water.

3. In a separate bowl, mix remaining Filling ingredients.

4. Add the baking soda and hot water mixture to the Filling and mix.

5. Allow to cool while you make the Crumbs.

6. In a medium bowl, mix Crumbs ingredients together until coarse crumbs appear.

7. Stir 3½ cups Crumbs into Filling mixture.

8. Pour Filling into pie crusts.

9. Top with remaining Crumbs.

10. Bake at 350°F for 50 minutes or until dry and crumbly on top.

CHOCOLATE SHOOFLY PIE

Yield: 2 (9-inch) pies

Ingredients:

2 (9-inch) pie crusts

Pudding:

1¼ cups sugar
2¼ tablespoons all-purpose flour
1½ tablespoons cornstarch
3 tablespoons cocoa
3 tablespoons butter

Topping:

1 egg
1 cup vegetable shortening
¾ cup brown sugar
½ cup white sugar
1 cup molasses
1 cup hot water
2½ cups all-purpose flour
1¼ tablespoons cocoa
1 teaspoon baking soda
½ teaspoon salt
Frosting of choice (optional)

Instructions:

1. Roll out pie crusts and place in pie plates.

2. Mix all Pudding ingredients in a saucepan.

3. Heat over medium heat, stirring often until thickened.

4. Cool completely.

5. Pour into bottom of two pie crusts.

6. Preheat oven to 350°F.

7. In a large bowl, mix all Topping ingredients.

8. Divide Topping evenly over the two pies.

9. Bake at 350°F for one hour.

10. Cool pies completely.

11. If you want, frost with your favorite chocolate or vanilla icing. I use a traditional buttercream frosting recipe.

Recipe Note: To make chocolate buttercream frosting, beat 6 tablespoons room temperature butter until light and fluffy. Gradually add ½ cup cocoa powder, beating slowly to incorporate the cocoa powder. Gradually add ⅓ cup milk and 1 teaspoon vanilla extract, continuing to beat. Add 2½ cups confectioners' sugar a little at a time, beating until smooth. For thicker frosting, add more confectioners' sugar. To thin it out, add a bit more milk.

BUTTERSCOTCH PIE

Yield: 1 (8-inch) pie

Ingredients:

1 (8-inch) bottom pie crust or graham cracker crust, baked

Filling:
2 tablespoons butter
1 cup brown sugar
½ cup hot water
½ teaspoon salt
2 egg yolks
2 tablespoons all-purpose flour
2 tablespoons cornstarch
2 cups evaporated milk
Whipped cream, for serving

Instructions:

1. Brown the butter: Place butter in a saucepan and melt over medium heat. Stir with a spatula as the butter bubbles and foams. When the butter begins to smell nutty, move to the next step.

2. Add brown sugar and water and allow to simmer, bubbling lightly, for a few minutes. Remove from heat.

3. Add remaining ingredients and beat well.

4. Return to heat and heat until thickened, stirring often.

5. Pour into pie crust.

6. Cool and top with whipped cream.

OATMEAL PIE

Yield: 1 (9-inch) pie

Ingredients:

1 (9-inch) bottom pie crust, unbaked

Filling:

3 eggs, beaten
1 cup heavy cream
1 cup corn syrup
1 teaspoon vanilla extract
1 tablespoon all-purpose flour
¼ teaspoon salt
1 cup quick oats
½ cup chopped nuts (optional)

Instructions:

1. Roll out pie crust and place in pie plate.
2. Preheat oven to 350°F.
3. Mix all Filling ingredients, stirring well.
4. Pour into unbaked pie crust.
5. Bake at 350°F for 45 minutes.

COCONUT OATMEAL PIE

Yield: 2 (8-inch) pies

Ingredients:

2 (8-inch) bottom pie crusts, unbaked

Filling:

1½ cups corn syrup
1½ cups brown sugar
¾ cup melted butter
½ cup water
¼ teaspoon baking soda
4 eggs, beaten
½ cup coconut, sweetened
½ cup pecan or walnuts, chopped
1½ cups quick oats

Instructions:

1. Roll out pie crusts and place in 8-inch pie plates.

2. Preheat oven to 425°F.

3. Mix all Filling ingredients.

4. Divide between two unbaked pie crusts.

5. Bake at 425°F for 10 minutes.

6. Reduce heat to 375°F and continue baking 25 minutes.

Recipe Note: This was another pie Grandma was famous for. I liked it so well, we asked her to bake it for our wedding. She was more than happy to oblige; nothing pleased Grandma more than to feed people and receive compliments for her food.

SWEET POTATO PIE (VARIATION #1)

Yield: 1 (9-inch) pie

Ingredients:

1 (9-inch) bottom pie crust

Filling:

⅓ cup butter, softened
½ cup brown sugar
¾ cup heavy cream
2 cups mashed, cooked sweet potatoes
1½ teaspoons vanilla extract
1 teaspoon cinnamon
½ teaspoon salt

Whipped cream, for serving

Instructions:

1. Roll out bottom pie crust and place in pie plate.

2. Preheat oven to 425°F.

3. Mix all Filling ingredients.

4. Pour into pie crust.

5. Bake at 425°F for 15 minutes.

6. Reduce heat to 350°F and continue baking 40 minutes.

7. Cool and serve with whipped cream.

SWEET POTATO PIE (VARIATION #2)

Yield: 1 (9-inch) pie

Ingredients:

1 (9-inch) bottom pie crust, unbaked
2 eggs
1 (12-ounce) can evaporated milk
1 teaspoon vanilla extract
1¾ cups sugar
1 teaspoon cinnamon
½ teaspoon nutmeg
1½ cups cooked, mashed sweet potatoes

Instructions:

1. Roll out pie crust and place in pie plate.

2. Preheat oven to 375°F.

3. Beat eggs.

4. Stir in evaporated milk, vanilla extract, sugar, and spices.

5. Add the sweet potatoes and beat well until filling mixture is smooth.

6. Pour filling into the pie crust.

7. Bake at 375°F for 50 minutes.

Savory Pies

Tomato Pie   **127**

Potato Pie   **128**

Chicken Pie   **131**

TOMATO PIE

Yield: 1 (9-inch) pie

Ingredients:

1 (9-inch) crust, unbaked
8–10 tomatoes, sliced
¾ cup mayonnaise
½–¾ cup cheese (cheddar, provolone, or mozzarella)
¼ cup chopped onions (optional)
1 teaspoon oregano
¼ teaspoon garlic salt
¼–½ teaspoon pepper
Bacon crumbles (optional)

Instructions:

1. Roll out pie crust and place in pie plate.

2. Preheat oven to 350°F.

3. Slice tomatoes and place slices on a paper towel to drain.

4. Combine mayo, cheese, onions, and seasonings.

5. Arrange ⅓ of tomato slices in bottom of crust.

6. Spread with cheese mixture.

7. Repeat layers until tomatoes and cheese are all used up.

8. Bake at 350°F for 25 minutes or until bubbly.

9. Sprinkle with bacon.

Recipe Note: this is my favorite savory pie. I usually make mine without bacon, and if I have fresh oregano and basil, I use that. Basil adds a delicious flavor! You can also add herbs to the crust of any savory pie. It looks pretty and tastes great!

POTATO PIE

Yield: 1 (9-inch) pie

Ingredients:

Crust:
1½ cups mashed potatoes
⅓ cup milk or sour cream
1½ tablespoons all-purpose flour
1 teaspoon baking powder
1 egg
Salt and pepper, to taste
2 tablespoons melted butter

Filling:
2 eggs
1 cup heavy cream
Salt and pepper, to taste
½ cup cheddar cheese

Instructions:

1. Preheat oven to 350°F and grease a 9-inch pie pan.

2. Combine all Crust ingredients and press into greased pie pan.

3. Combine all Filling ingredients and pour into prepared crust.

4. Bake at 350°F for 20 to 25 minutes or until golden brown.

Recipe Note: Potato pie is a great way to use leftover mashed potatoes.

CHICKEN PIE

Yield: 1 (9-inch) pie

Ingredients:

1 (9-inch) top and bottom pie crust, unbaked
1 tablespoon butter
3 tablespoons all-purpose flour
1 quart chicken broth or stock
  (homemade stock is great!)
1 cup cooked chicken, cut in bite-size pieces
1 cup cooked, diced potatoes
½–¾ cup cooked, diced celery
½–¾ cup cooked, diced carrots
½ cup cooked, diced onions
Salt and pepper, to taste

Instructions:

1. Roll out crust and place in pie plate.

2. Preheat oven to 350°F.

3. Melt butter in a saucepan, add flour, and whisk to make a roux.

4. Slowly add broth, whisking until smooth, and then add remaining ingredients.

5. Pour into pie shell.

6. Top with pie crust.

7. Bake at 350°F for 30 minutes or until bubbly and golden brown.

Recipe Note: Chicken pie is the most popular savory pie in Amish circles. It's a common fundraiser product as well, sold frozen—they always sell well! Most recipes for chicken pie include the same ingredients; the only variation is the seasonings.

INDEX

A

Apple Crumb Pie, 18
Apple Pie, 17
applesauce
    Snitz Pies, 49

B

bacon
    Tomato Pie, 127
berries
    Fresh Fruit Pie, 21
blueberries
    Fresh Blueberry Pie, 26
Butterscotch Pie, 115

C

Cappuccino Ice Cream Pie, 94
carrots
    Chicken Pie, 131
celery
    Chicken Pie, 131
cereal
    rice
        Frozen Strawberry Pie
            (Variation #1), 53
        Ice Cream "Pie" with Peanut
            Butter Crust, 93

cheese
    cheddar
        Potato Pie, 128
        Tomato Pie, 127
cherries
    Fresh Fruit Pie, 21
Chicken Pie, 131
Chocolate Chess Pie, 100
Chocolate Chip Cookie Pie, 103
Chocolate Oatmeal Pie, 119
Chocolate Pie, 99
Chocolate Shoofly Pie, 112
cinnamon
    Apple Crumb Pie, 18
    Apple Pie, 17
    Cappuccino Ice Cream Pie, 94
    Graham Cracker Crusts, 10
Grandma's Pumpkin Pie, 38
    Layered Pumpkin Pie, 46
    Pear Custard Pie, 78
    Pear Pie, 58
    Plum Pie, 57
    Pumpkin Pie (Variation #1), 41
    Pumpkin Pie (Variation #2), 42
    Pumpkin Pie (Variation #3), 45
    Shoofly Pie (Variation #1), 108
    Snitz Pies, 49

Sweet Potato Pie (Variation
    #1), 120
Sweet Potato Pie (Variation
    #2), 123
Clear-jel
    Fresh Fruit Pie, 21
cocoa
    Chocolate Chess Pie, 100
    Chocolate Pie, 99
    Chocolate Shoofly Pie, 112
    Peanut Butter Cup Pies, 72
coconut
    Chocolate Oatmeal Pie, 119
coffee, instant
    Cappuccino Ice Cream Pie, 94
cookie crumbs
    Cookie Crust, 13
    Peanut Butter Pie with
        Chocolate Crust, 71
Cookie Crust, 13
    Frozen Strawberry Pie
        (Variation #2), 54
cream cheese
    Easy Peanut Butter Pie, 68
    Frozen Strawberry Pie
        (Variation #2), 54
    Peaches and Cream Pie, 81

Peanut Butter Cup Pies, 72
Peanut Butter Pie with
    Chocolate Crust, 71
Pear Custard Pie, 78
Raspberry Swirl Pie, 82
Cream Cheese Pecan Pie, 90
crusts
    Cookie Crust, 13
    Graham Cracker Crusts, 10
    Oatmeal Crust, 8

D
dough, 3, 4, 7. *See also* crusts

E
Easy Peanut Butter Pie, 68

F
French Rhubarb Pie, 29
Fresh Blueberry Pie, 26
Fresh Fruit Pie, 21
Fresh Peach Pie, 25
Fresh Strawberry Pie, 22
Frozen Strawberry Pie (Variation
    #1), 53
Frozen Strawberry Pie (Variation
    #2), 54
fudge topping
    Cappuccino Ice Cream Pie, 94

G
ginger
    Pumpkin Pie (Variation #2), 42
Graham Cracker Crusts, 10
    Butterscotch Pie, 115
    Cappuccino Ice Cream Pie, 94
    Easy Peanut Butter Pie, 68
    Fresh Blueberry Pie, 26

Fresh Peach Pie, 25
Fresh Strawberry Pie, 22
Frozen Strawberry Pie
    (Variation #2), 54
Raspberry Swirl Pie, 82
Grandma's Pecan Pie, 64
Grandma's Pumpkin Pie, 38

I
Ice Cream "Pie" with Peanut
    Butter Crust, 93

J
jell-O
    apricot
        Fresh Peach Pie, 25
    peach
        Fresh Peach Pie, 25
    raspberry
        Fresh Strawberry Pie, 22
    strawberry
        Fresh Strawberry Pie, 22

L
Layered Pumpkin Pie, 46
Lemon Meringue Pie, 33
Lemon Sponge Pie, 34

M
Maple Cream Pie, 89
mayonnaise
    Tomato Pie, 127
molasses
    Layered Pumpkin Pie, 46
    Pumpkin Pie (Variation #1), 41
    Shoofly Pie (Variation #1), 108
    Shoofly Pie (Variation #2), 111
    Vanilla Pie, 104

N
nutmeg
    Pumpkin Pie (Variation #2), 42
    Pumpkin Pie (Variation #3), 45
    Sweet Potato Pie (Variation
        #2), 123

O
oatmeal
    Chocolate Oatmeal Pie, 119
    Strawberry Rhubarb Crumb
        Pie, 50
Oatmeal Crust, 8
Oatmeal Pie, 116
    Chocolate Oatmeal Pie, 119
onions
    Chicken Pie, 131
    Tomato Pie, 127
oregano
    Tomato Pie, 127

P
peaches
    Fresh Fruit Pie, 21
Peaches and Cream Pie, 81
peanut butter
    Easy Peanut Butter Pie, 68
    Frozen Strawberry Pie
        (Variation #1), 53
    Ice Cream "Pie" with Peanut
        Butter Crust, 93
    Peanut Butter Pie with
        Chocolate Crust, 71
Peanut Butter Cup Pies, 72
Peanut Butter Pie with Chocolate
    Crust, 71
Pear Custard Pie, 78
Pear Pie, 58

pears
    Fresh Fruit Pie, 21
    Sour Cream Pear Pie, 77
Pecan Pie
    Grandma's Pecan Pie, 64
    Variation #1, 63
    Variation #3, 67
pecans
    Apple Crumb Pie, 18
    Chocolate Oatmeal Pie, 119
    Cream Cheese Pecan Pie, 90
    Maple Cream Pie, 89
    Raisin Cream Pie (Variation
      #2), 86
Pie Dough, 3, 4, 7
pies
    chocolate
      Chocolate Chess Pie, 100
      Chocolate Chip Cookie Pie,
        103
      Chocolate Pie, 99
      Chocolate Shoofly Pie, 112
    cream
      Cream Cheese Pecan Pie, 90
      Maple Cream Pie, 89
      Peaches and Cream Pie, 81
      Pear Custard Pie, 78
      Raisin Cream Pie (Variation
        #2), 86
      Raisin Crème Pie (Variation
        #1), 85
      Raspberry Swirl Pie, 82
      Sour Cream Pear Pie, 77
    fruit
      Apple Crumb Pie, 18
      Apple Pie, 17
      French Rhubarb Pie, 29
      Fresh Blueberry Pie, 26
      Fresh Fruit Pie, 21

Fresh Peach Pie, 25
Fresh Strawberry Pie, 22
Frozen Strawberry Pie
  (Variation #1), 53
Frozen Strawberry Pie
  (Variation #2), 54
Grandma's Pumpkin Pie, 38
Lemon Meringue Pie, 33
Lemon Sponge Pie, 34
Pear Pie, 58
Plum Pie, 57
Rhubarb Custard Pie, 30
Snitz Pies, 49
Sour Cream Lemon Pie,
  37
Strawberry Rhubarb Crumb
  Pie, 50
ice cream
    Cappuccino Ice Cream Pie,
      94
    Ice Cream "Pie" with Peanut
      Butter Crust, 93
nut
    Easy Peanut Butter Pie, 68
    Grandma's Pecan Pie, 64
    Peanut Butter Cup Pies, 72
    Peanut Butter Pie with
      Chocolate Crust, 71
    Pecan Pie (Variation #1), 63
    Pecan Pie (Variation #3), 67
savory
    Chicken Pie, 131
    Tomato Pie, 127
vanilla
    Vanilla Crumb Pie, 107
    Vanilla Pie, 104
Plum Pie, 57
potatoes
    Chicken Pie, 131

sweet
    Sweet Potato Pie (Variation
      #1), 120
    Sweet Potato Pie (Variation
      #2), 123
Potato Pie, 128
pudding
    vanilla
      Peaches and Cream Pie, 81
pumpkin
    Pumpkin Pie (Variation #2), 42
    Pumpkin Pie (Variation #3), 45
    Pumpkin Pie (Variation #1), 41
    Pumpkin Pie (Variation #2), 42
    Pumpkin Pie (Variation #3), 45
pumpkin purée
    Grandma's Pumpkin Pie, 38
    Layered Pumpkin Pie, 46
    Pumpkin Pie (Variation #1), 41

R
Raisin Cream Pie (Variation #2),
  86
Raisin Crème Pie (Variation #1),
  85
Raspberry Swirl Pie, 82
rhubarb
    French Rhubarb Pie, 29
    Rhubarb Custard Pie, 30
    Strawberry Rhubarb Crumb
      Pie, 50
Rhubarb Custard Pie, 30

S
Shoofly Pie
  (Variation #1), 108
  (Variation #2), 111
  Chocolate Shoofly Pie, 112
Snitz Pies, 49

Sour Cream Lemon Pie, 37
Sour Cream Pear Pie, 77
strawberries
    Fresh Strawberry Pie, 22
    Frozen Strawberry Pie
        (Variation #1), 53
    Frozen Strawberry Pie
        (Variation #2), 54
    Strawberry Rhubarb Crumb
        Pie, 50
strawberry jam
    Raspberry Swirl Pie, 82
Strawberry Rhubarb Crumb Pie,
    50
Sweet Potato Pie (Variation #1),
    120
Sweet Potato Pie (Variation #2),
    123

T
tapioca
    Snitz Pies, 49
Tomato Pie, 127

V
Vanilla Crumb Pie, 107
Vanilla Pie, 104

W
walnuts
    Chocolate Oatmeal Pie, 119
    Maple Cream Pie, 89
    Raisin Cream Pie (Variation
        #2), 86
whipped topping
    Chocolate Pie, 99
    Easy Peanut Butter Pie, 68

Fresh Peach Pie, 25
Fresh Strawberry Pie, 22
Frozen Strawberry Pie
    (Variation #1), 53
Frozen Strawberry Pie
    (Variation #2), 54
Maple Cream Pie, 89
Peanut Butter Cup Pies, 72
Raisin Cream Pie (Variation
    #2), 86
Raisin Crème Pie (Variation
    #1), 85

METRIC CONVERSIONS

If you're accustomed to using metric measurements, use these handy charts to convert the imperial measurements used in this book.

Weight (Dry Ingredients)

1 oz		30 g
4 oz	¼ lb	120 g
8 oz	½ lb	240 g
12 oz	¾ lb	360 g
16 oz	1 lb	480 g
32 oz	2 lb	960 g

Oven Temperatures

Fahrenheit	Celsius	Gas Mark
225°	110°	¼
250°	120°	½
275°	140°	1
300°	150°	2
325°	160°	3
350°	180°	4
375°	190°	5
400°	200°	6
425°	220°	7
450°	230°	8

Volume (Liquid Ingredients)

½ tsp.		2 ml
1 tsp.		5 ml
1 Tbsp.	½ fl oz	15 ml
2 Tbsp.	1 fl oz	30 ml
¼ cup	2 fl oz	60 ml
⅓ cup	3 fl oz	80 ml
½ cup	4 fl oz	120 ml
⅔ cup	5 fl oz	160 ml
¾ cup	6 fl oz	180 ml
1 cup	8 fl oz	240 ml
1 pt	16 fl oz	480 ml
1 qt	32 fl oz	960 ml

Length

¼ in	6 mm
½ in	13 mm
¾ in	19 mm
1 in	25 mm
6 in	15 cm
12 in	30 cm

ALSO AVAILABLE

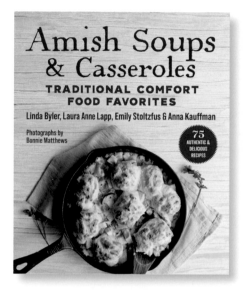

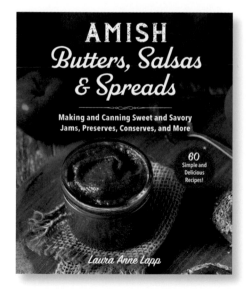

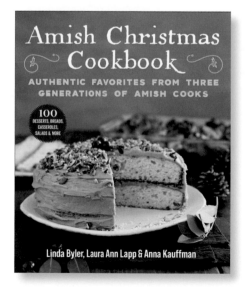